# CURLING

JAMES S. MITCHEL

COMPLETE RULES AND REGULATIONS,
WITH DIAGRAMS OF PLAY

REVISED FOR 1899

Published by Left of Brain Books

ISBN 978-1-396-31820-7

*First Edition*

# Table of Contents

# CURLING.

"Noo, fill a bumper to the brim,
And drink wi' three times three, man;
May curlers on life's slippery rink
Trae crul rubs be free, man."

The game of curling is one of the most interesting of our winter amusements. While the majority are inclined to look on the features of the sport in a jocose light, yet we think that it affords scope for a display of skill, such as few games demand; in fact, it has been claimed that no mortal can curl to perfection, but tradition has it that a certain Tam Pate, who flourished in the early part of this century, never missed a shot.

Of the origin of curling it is hard to speak with accuracy, for in every European country where civilization has entered, their annals speak of it in some shape or other. It drifted about from clime to clime until it finally found home in the bosom of Scotland.

But by far the most important event in the history of curling was the formation of the Grand Caledonian Club in 1838. In 1843 the word *Royal* was added by orders of Her Majesty on a visit to Scotland, and since the club has numbered amongst its presidents His R. H., the Prince of Wales, as well as other members of the Royal Family, the game now is so thoroughly Scotch that it cannot adapt itself to the language and manners of any other country. Wherever a curling pond is to be found, a Scotchman is to be found at the bottom of it, and the game will not be universal until Scotch is the one tongue, and the human race one Scotch family—an event, however desirable to some, is not a probable occurrence.

In 1878 the Rusholme Ice Rink, at Manchester, was constructed at a cost of £20,000. The Southport Glaciarium followed in 1879 at a cost of £30,0000. The cause of these expensive rinks was want of natural ice, owing to the mildness of the climate.

Curling was introduced into Ireland by the Scotch adventurers, who were sent across as planters to root in the soil and undermine the native buds. However, all traces of the sport had disappeared when Dr. Carnie formed the Belfast Club in 1839.

The game has gone forth and fared better. In Canada, where ice and Scotch settlers prevail, curling is a favorite sport. There are now nineteen clubs in the Quebec province, all affiliated to the Royal Club.

In 1874 curling had made such progress in Western Canada that the Ontario province was formed separate, with its headquarters at Toronto.

Curlers in the United Stated have also since 1867 been organized under a grand national club with its headquarters in New York.

A footing has also been obtained by the roaming game in New Zealand, Newfoundland, Nova Scotia, Russia, Norway and in Switzerland.

The following table shows the distribution of clubs and curlers:

|                   | Clubs | Members |
|-------------------|-------|---------|
| Scotland          | 481   | 18,800  |
| England           | 33    | 1,607   |
| Ireland           | 3     | 64      |
| Norway            | 1     | 15      |
| Russia            | 1     | 26      |
| New Zealand       | 6     | 193     |
| Quebec Province   | 19    | 1,081   |
| Ontario Province  | 99    | 3,551   |
| Manitoba          | 18    | 810     |
| Nova Scotia       | 7     | 287     |
| Newfoundland      | 3     | 89      |
| New Brunswick     | 3     | 155     |
| United States     | 40    | 800     |
| Total             | 714   | 26,978  |

The most important article in the curler's outfit is the curling stone. In selecting a pair of stones the curler should not omit to take the beauty of the article into account, although it must not, of course, be preferred to real worth. Let him remember that the stone must be his servant, not his master, and select one over which he has command. It is also good to bear in mind that the best assistant in the management of the stone is *polish*. The careful curler will never allow his curling stone to loose its gloss or brilliancy. With this the heaviest stone is easily managed; without it the lightest stone is dull, stubborn and unmanageable. What the curler requires is a true stone—*i.e.* a stone which will not be dull when the ice is dull and keen when the ice is keen, but which will be equable in mood and not affected by change of weather. Those on sale by A. G. Spalding & Bros., Broadway, New York, are far superior to any I have seen imported or otherwise.

It will thus be seen that the rink game is in the hands of a skip or director. The essential qualities of this worthy is, that he should have a thorough knowledge of the game. He must be a man of humor, delighting in jokes and jollities. With a couple of sour skips at the end of the rink all the life goes out of the game. A skip should be a man of imperturbable temper, never put out when a mishap occurs, never blaming anybody, never angry at his men, never blaming anybody but himself, in the hour of defeat unmurmuring, and in the hour of triumph generous. He must be just, honest, wise, cool, prudent, watchful, brave, courageous and blameless as a bishop. By the tee, watching and directing, he should stand. He should know what each of his team has to perform, as each has his place to fill. It is four against four battling round the tee seeing who first will take it, and who last will hold it. The first player, with a pair of heavy stones, must draw up toward the coveted spot. The second must protect the *lead* if the enemy has not dislodged him. The third, most likely, have an angular wick or cannon-shot to play.

The next important feature of the sport, is the *position*. In rule 1, distinct instruction is given as to the place of the crampit on which the player is to take his stand. He must *fit the tee*, i.e., he must so place himself that his eye travels along the central line toward the farther tee, while his right foot rests in the hack or on the heel of the crampit. No matter what kind of a shot he may be asked to play, even though the point aimed at maybe several feet to the right or to the left of the distant tee, the crampit or hack is immovable, and no advantage must be taken by changing to a place from which the shot could be more easily taken. A player need never trouble himself about the awkwardness of his position if he find that he has command of his stone, and can always do the needful when his skip gives the word of command.

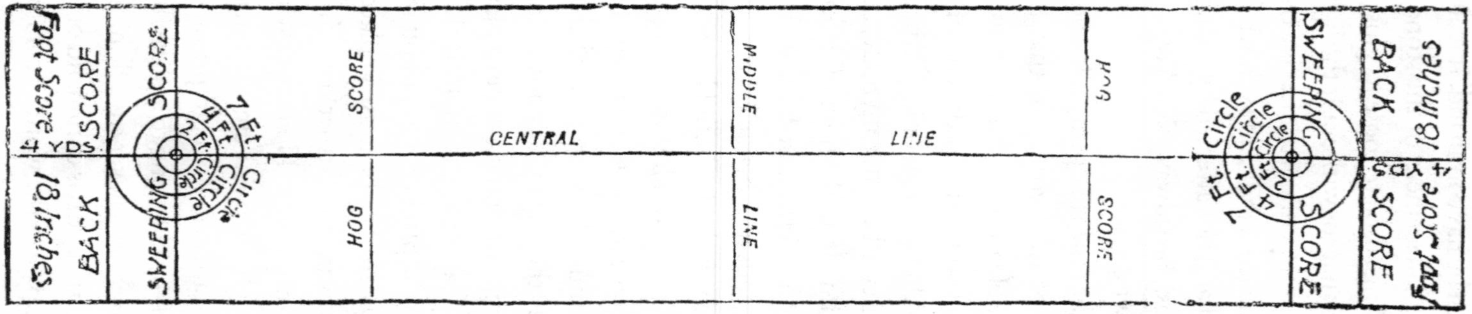

DIAGRAM OF CURLING RUNK

Foot Score    4 YDS    18 Inches
BACK        SCORE

SWEEPING    SCORE
7 Ft. Circle
4 Ft. Circle
2 Ft. Circle

HOG        SCORE

CENTRAL    LINE

MIDDLE    LINE

SCORE        HOG

7 Ft. Circle
4 Ft. Circle
2 Ft. Circle
SWEEPING    SCORE

SCORE    4 YDS    BACK
Foot Score    18 Inches

The *swing* now requires attention. Hutchinson says that the curling stone should describe the same figure in its upward journey as you hope to make it describe in its descent. As the stone descends, the centre of gravity is advanced, and the left foot must also be lifted and advanced as a base-line to preserve the stability of the body. This saves one from rushing forward along the ice. The lifting of the left foot gives freedom in swinging the body and arm to the right or left, as the mark to be aimed at may require, for such movement is necessary and does not interfere with the first duty of *fitting the tee*. One of the worst faults in curling is a clumsy, awkward *delivery* of the stone. By this the ice alongside the crampit is cracked and broken up, and the curler gives much annoyance to the other players, besides he does himself injury. When a stone is quietly and gracefully delivered, it is far more effective than a stone played with double energy, the force of which is half spent by the blow it receives as it meets the ice.

But the most important of all is the *twist*, or what has been termed the acme of the curling art. This is the accomplishment which gives a finishing touch to curling proficiency, and differentiates the truly scientific player from all his brethren, however keen. By putting "twist" on the stone it can be made to curl against the bias altogether, while the stone of the straight player is helplessly at its mercy. It is even useful to know the twist when a straight shot has to be played, for in delivering the stone the player is apt, unconsciously, to give the stone a curl of some kind, a curl that he perhaps does not wish to give it. This the practiced hand can avoid. Just as in bowling, the skip is accustomed to indicate to the player whether the bias or lead of the bowl be "in" or "out," and how much green he is to take, so in curling the skip often calls "elbow in" or "elbow out" as required, and points to where the player is to lay on or design for, that with the curl the shot may be taken. Without such directions, if a player only knows what is to be done he ought to know what twist to put on, and how to negotiate the business for himself without any such directions.

# RULES FOR CURLING—RINK MEDALS.

Sec. I. The length of the rink played shall be forty-two yards. The tees shall be put down thirty-eight yards apart. In a continued straight line with the tees, and four yards distant from each, a circle, eighteen inches in diameter, shall be drawn on the left-hand side of said line (looking in the direction to be played), and its edge just touching it. Within this circle, whether standing on the ice, or on any rest, support, or abutment whatsoever, permitted by the rules, each player, when playing his stone, shall place his right foot and his left foot on the left-hand side of the central line (the circle to be on the opposite side of the line if the player be left-handed). When a hack or hatch in the ice is used, it must be behind the circle above described, and not of greater length than fourteen inches, measuring from the central line. A circle of seven feet radius to be described from each tee as a centre to, and no stone to count which passes this, and beyond a line drawn across the further edge of the seven-feet circle; such stone to be treated as out of the game, and put off the ice. Should this be neglected, and another stone stopped against it, and within seven feet of the tee, the stone so stopped to be counted in the game. The hog-score to be distant from each tee one-sixth part of the whole rink played. Every one to be a hog which does not clear a square placed upon this score but no stone to be considered a hog which has struck another stone lying over the hog-score. A line shall be drawn on the ice at right angles to the rink, half-way between the tees, which shall be called "The Middle Line". In no case shall the rink played be less than thirty-two yards.

As soon as the rink is marked off, and before beginning to play, the terms of the match or game must be distinctly stated and fixed by the skips, if they have not been previously arranged. These terms may either be, that the parties shall play for a specified time, or a game of a certain number of shots or heads. Though the terms have been previously fixed, they should here be repeated.

Sec. 2. Every rink to be composed of four players a side, each with two stones. Before commencing the game, each skip shall state to his opposing skip the rotation in which his men are to play, and the rotation so fixed is not to be changed during the game. Each pair of players shall play one stone alternately with his opponent, till he has played both.

Sec. 3. The two skips opposing each other shall settle by lot, or any other way they may agree upon, which party shall lead, after which the winning party of the last end shall do so.

Sec. 4. All curling stones shall be of a circular shape. No stone shall be of a greater weight than forty-four pounds imperial, nor less than thirty-two pounds, nor of greater circumference than thirty-six inches, nor of less height than one-eighth part of its greatest circumference, unless the club uses iron blocks. No iron block to exceed over seventy pounds in weight. And the same rules as to size must govern the iron blocks which govern the stones. Players may change the side of their stones once during the game, but they shall not be allowed to change them oftener, or change stones after the commencement of the game, unless by mutual consent of the skips, except one or both may be broken, and then the largest portion of the broken stone to count, without any necessity for playing with it more. If the played stone rolls and stops on its side or top, it shall not be counted, but put off the ice. Should the handle quit the stone in the delivery, the player must keep hold of it, otherwise he shall not be entitled to replay his shot.

Sec. 5. Each party, before beginning to play, and during the course of each end, to be arranged along the sides of the rink, anywhere between the middle line and the tee which their skip may direct; but no party, except when sweeping according to the rule, shall go upon the middle of the rink, nor cross it under any pretence whatever. The skips alone to stand at or about the tee, as their turn requires.

Sec. 6. If a player plays out of turn, the stone so played may be stopped in its progress, and returned to the player. If the mistake shall not be discovered till the stone is again at rest, the opposite party shall have the option to add one to their score, and the game proceed in its original rotation, or to declare the end null and void.

Sec. 7. The sweeping department shall be under the exclusive direction and control of the skips. The player's party shall be allowed to sweep when the stone is past the middle line, and till it reaches the tee; the adverse party, when it has passed the tee. The sweeping to be always to a side or across the rink; and no sweepings to be moved forward and left in front of a running stone, so as to stop or obstruct its course. Either party may sweep behind the tee, before or after the stone has been played, or while in motion.

Sec. 8. If in sweeping or otherwise a running stone be marred by any of the party to which it belongs, it shall be put off the ice; if by any of the adverse party, it shall be placed where the skip of the party to which it belongs shall direct. If marred by any other means the player shall replay his stone. Should any played stone be accidentally displaced by any of the opposing party before the last stone is played, for the first offence it shall be replaced by the skip to whom it belongs in as near its original position as possible before it was displaced; and for the second offence by the same party, the opposing party shall have the privilege of declaring the end null and void, or of replacing the stone. If a played stone is moved accidentally by any of the party to whom it belongs, it shall be in the decision of the opposing skip to replace the stone as nearly as possible to where it was before being moved, or to allow it to remain where it was accidentally moved to. No stone displaced by either party shall be allowed to be moved if it has been struck or moved by a running stone, before the claim for moving has been made.

Sec. 9. Each player to come provided with a besom, to be ready to play when his turn comes, and not to take more than a reasonable time to play his stone. Should he accidentally play a wrong stone, any of the players may stop it while running; if not stopped till it is again at rest, it shall be replaced by the one which he ought to have played.

Sec. 10. No measuring of shots allowed previous to the termination of the end. Disputed shots to be determined by the skips, or, if they disagree, by the umpire; or, when there is no umpire, by some neutral person mutually chosen by them, whose decision shall be final. All measurements to be taken from the centre of the tee, to the part of the stone which is nearest to it. No stone shall be considered within or without a circle unless it clear it and every stone shall be held as resting on a line which does not completely clear it—in every case that is to be determined by placing a square on the ice at that part of the circle or line in dispute.

Sec. 11. Each skip shall have the exclusive regulation and direction of the game for his party, and may play in what part of it he pleases; but having chosen his place at the beginning, he must retain it till the end of the game but no skip, when his turn to play comes, after having appointed one of his party to take charge for him, shall be allowed after leaving the ice to go back and examine the end, but shall take directions from the party appointed by himself. The players may give their advice, but cannot control their director; nor are they, upon any pretext, to address themselves to the person about to play. Each skip, when his own turn to play comes, shall name one of his party to take charge for him. Every player to follow implicitly the directions given him. If any player shall improperly speak to, taunt or interrupt another while in the act of delivering his stone, one shot shall be added to the score of the party interrupted, and the end proceed as before.

Sec. 12. If from any change of weather, after a game has been begun, or from any other reasonable cause whatsoever, one party shall desire to shorten the rink, or to change to another one, and if the two skips cannot agree upon it, the umpire for the occasion shall be called, and he shall, after seeing one end played, determine whether the rink shall be shortened, and how much, or whether it shall be changed, and his determination shall be final and binding on all parties. Should there be no umpire appointed for the occasion, or should he be otherwise engaged, the two skips may call in any curler unconnected with the disputing parties whose services can most readily be got, and subject to the same conditions; his power shall be equally extensive as the umpire aforesaid.

Sec. 13. Should any question arise, the determination of which is not provided for by the words and spirit of the rules now established, it may be referred to the Executive Committee.

NOTE.—In all these preliminary drawings and descriptions, distinct reference is to be made to the terms used in the prefixed diagram or plan called "The Rink."

# RULES FOR LOCAL COMPETITION.
## POINT GAME.

1. Competitors shall draw lots for rotation of play, and shall use two stones.

2. The length of the rink shall not exceed 42 yards; any lesser distance shall be determined by the umpire.

3. Circles of 7 feet and 4 feet radius shall be drawn round the tee, and a central line through the centre of the 4-foot circle to the hog-score.

4. Every competitor shall play four shots at each of the eight following points of the game, viz.: Striking, inwicking, drawing, guarding, chap and lie, wick and curl in, raising and chipping the winner, according to the following definition (See diagram next page):

5. In Nos 2, 6, 8 and 9, two chances on the left and two on the right.

DIAGRAM TO BE DRAWN ON THE ICE PREVIOUS TO PLAYING.[1]

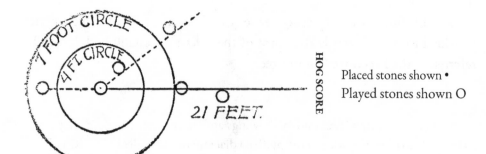

Placed stones shown •
Played stones shown O

---

[1] NOTE.—It will save much time if in playing local matches, two rinks be prepared lying parallel to each other, the tee of the one being at the reverse end of the other rink, every competitor play both stones up the one rink, and immediately after wards both down the other, finishing thus at each round all the chances at that point. It will also save time if a code of signals be arranged between tho marker and the players, such as, the marker to raise one hand when 1 is scored, and both hands when 2 are scored. In case of a miss hands to be kept down.

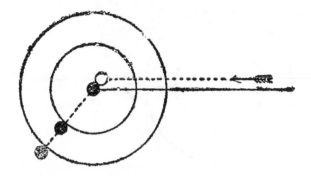

1. *Striking.*—A stone placed on the tee. If struck, to count 1; if struck out of the 7-foot circle, to count 2.

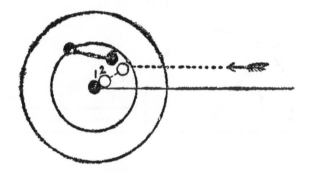

2. *Inwicking.*—A stone being placed on the tee, and another with its inner edge 2 feet 6 inches from the tee, and its fore edge on a line drawn from the tee at an angle of 45° with the central line.

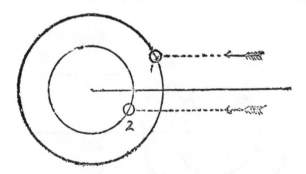

3. *Drawing.*—If the stone played lies within or on the 7-foot circle, to count 1; if within or on the 4 -foot circle, to count 2.

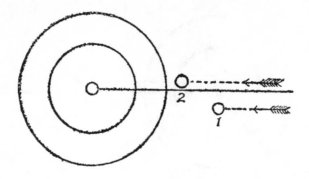

4. *Guarding.*—A stone placed on the tee. If the stone played rests within 6 inches of the central line, to count 1; if on the line, to count 2. It shall be over the hog, but not touch the stone to be guarded.

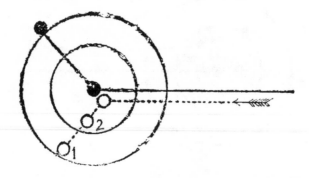

5. *Chap and Lie.*—If a stone placed on the tee be struck out of the 7-foot circle, and the played stone lie within or on the same circle, to count 1; if struck out of the 7-foot circle, and the played stone be within or on the 4-foot circle, to count 2.

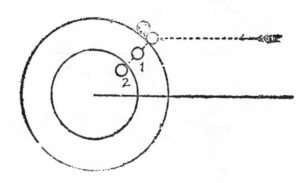

6. *Wick and Curl in.*—A stone being placed with its inner edge 7 feet distant from the tee, and its fore edge on a line, making an angle of 45° with the central line. If the stone is struck, and the played stone curls on or within the 7-foot circle, to count 1; if struck, and the played stone curls on or within the 4-foot circle, to count 2.

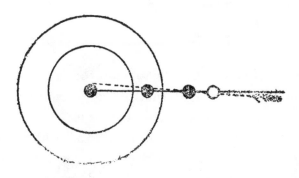

7. *Raising.*—A stone placed with its centre on the central line and its inner edge 8 feet distant from the tee. If struck into or on the 7-foot circle, to count 1; if struck into or on the 4-foot circle, to count 2.

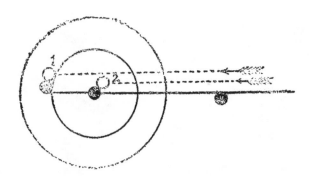

8. *Chipping the Winner.*—A stone being placed on the tee, and another with its inner edge 10 feet distant, just touching the central line, and half guarding the one on the tee, with its inner edge touching the central line, but on the opposite side from that on which the guard is placed. If the stone strikes the stone placed behind the tee, to count 1; if it strikes the stone on the tee, to count 2.

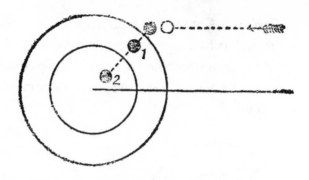

9. *Outwicking.*—In the event of two or more competitors gaining the same number of shots, they shall play for shots at *Outwicking*, that is, a stone being placed with its inner edge 7 feet distant from the tee, and its centre on a line, making an angle of 45° with the central line. If struck within or on the 7-foot circle, to count 1; if within or on the 4-foot circle, to count 2. If the competition cannot be decided with the shots, the umpire shall order one or more of the preceding points to be played again by the competitors equal.

CPSIA information can be obtained
at www.ICGtesting.com
Printed in the USA
BVHW031132230222
629769BV00020B/423